A is for Awkward

A Guide to
Surviving Middle School

By Aryelle Jacobsen

© 2017 by innerQuest, an imprint of Chiron Publications. All rights reserved. No part of this publication may be reproduced, stored in a retrieval system, or transmitted, in any form by any means, electronic, mechanical, photocopying, recording, or otherwise, without the prior written permission of the publisher, Chiron Publications, 932 Hendersonville Road, Suite 104, Asheville, North Carolina 28803.

Interior and cover design by Danijela Mijailovic
Printed primarily in the United States of America.

ISBN 978-1-63051-442-6 paperback
ISBN 978-1-63051-443-3 hardcover
ISBN 978-1-63051-444-0 electronic

Library of Congress Cataloging-in-Publication Data Pending

Published by innerQuest,
an imprint of Chiron Publications
innerQuestbooks.com
ChironPublications.com

Dedicated to
Jennifer Robinson;
a woman whose generosity,
friendship, and inspiration
made this project possible.

Love ya long time, J Rob.

Foreword
by
Olson Huff, MD

A is for Awkward.

A is also for Awesome.

In the vernacular of those caught between childhood and adolescence that is the best way to describe this book: Awesome!

Drawing from an intimate knowledge of the sometimes painful, often funny and ever present uncertainty of the "tween" years, this gem of a book is, itself, at times funny, revealing, poignant and enriching. Most of all, however, it is filled with wisdom that cradles the conflicting emotions of those having to endure middle school while simultaneously validating their right to claim their own identity.

Each letter of the alphabet introduces a theme to be absorbed, a lesson to live by and a reassurance that "hey, you are OK with who you are after all!"

Like "Chicken Soup for the Soul," this book is a primer designed to give hope, relieve fear, encourage expression and provide guidance for the journey through, yes, a very awkward time of life.

It should be treasured by and carried in the backpack of every one who embarks on that journey!

Olson Huff, MD is Founding Medical Director of Mission Children's Hospital and the Olson Huff Center for Child Development.

Acknowledgements

I wrote this book simply because I would have loved to have a resource like this when I was in middle school. This is advice from me and many of my friends who have experienced middle school and half of high school.
All the art incorporated in this book was drawn or painted by local teenagers. All my love and encouragement goes out to you in this extraordinarily awkward stage of life. Enjoy!

Authors: Aryelle Jacobsen,
Lauren Cavagnini, Samantha Zuniga

Illustrators: Aryelle Jacobsen,
Lauren Cavagnini, Samantha Zuniga,
Hannah Lancaster, Cade Brown, Isabela Ramirez, Kayleigh Needer, Grace Green, Gabe Poulos, Melody Shaffer, Adi Donahue

aisforawkwardbook@gmail.com
@aisforawkwardbook
A is for Awkward

A is for Awkward

I'll admit it, middle school
is an awkward time for everybody,
but that's okay.
This is a time to try new things,
learn from your mistakes,
meet new people, have fun,
and embrace that awkwardness
you'll find in yourself.
Enjoy every minute and
don't take it for granted.

B is for **Brave**

"All you need is 20 seconds of insane courage and I promise you something great will come out of it."
- *We Bought a Zoo*

I have personally found this quote to be very true. Bravery doesn't have to be some big action such as bungee jumping off a mountain. It can be little things like talking to the shy girl next to you on the first day of school. The little things in life always mean the most—so never be afraid, always be brave.

C is for Creativity

Creativity allows you
to express yourself by
drawing, writing, and much more
to relieve your feelings about
a certain situation.
Don't be afraid to let your
imagination take over and
let it all out. Sometimes
when I have a bad day
I come home and paint and
afterwards I feel 10 times better.
So give it a shot and
let your creativity flow!

D is for **Drama**

Like it or not, drama is bound to happen once you enter middle school. Sometimes you say something you regret, or someone says something about you behind your back. The best advice I can give is to always tell people how you feel in person, surround yourself with true friends, and never forget how far a genuine "sorry" can go. Remember that we all make mistakes and to always express your feelings.

E is for *Encouragement*

You never know how far
a kind gesture can go when
impacting someone's life.
A smile or a nice compliment
can make someone's day!
Encouragement in someone's
darkest hour always brightens
up their perspective and
can even help you. Finding the
good in others can always
help in finding
the good in yourself.

F is for **Friends**

When I was going into middle school, I was so afraid that I wouldn't make any friends because I was too shy. But the truth is, this is how the majority of kids feel when entering middle school.
I promise you'll develop great friendships with lots of different people. Some who will hold a special place in your heart forever.
I met my best friend in sixth grade and I can tell you she is still my best friend today.
Developing these friendships are important as they help you grow as a person and learn the values of trust.

G is for Grades don't define you

So maybe you're bummed because you got a D on your math test even though you spent endless hours of studying and memorizing equations. Well, I'll let you in on a little secret… this too shall pass. One bad grade isn't the end of the world and it doesn't define you. We all have unique talents that we embrace in different ways. Some of us are more talented in math, some are better in art. It all depends on what you're passionate about. All in all, at some point in time, you will fail a test. But I promise you that it will be okay.

H is for
HAVE FUN

Sure, it's always important
to lay back and relax once in
a while, but you'll never be as
young as you are at this very moment
in time. So take some risks,
go on adventures, let loose!
Never take what you have for
granted and have some fun.
Whether it's going on a hike,
reading a book, or having
a dance party, ask yourself,
"would I regret not
doing this?"

I is for
Intelligence

Intelligence is not defined by your grades, but by how you absorb and demonstrate the knowledge you have learned. Remember that we all have different strengths and weaknesses. Learning from others is a very commendable strength that takes dignity as well as humility. Being intelligent is not about comparing yourself to others, but tracking your own progress. Be gentle with yourself, we all illustrate intelligence in diverse ways.

J is for
JUST DO IT

This is one of the most simple yet powerful messages you can find. This motto doesn't only apply to sports but also to schoolwork, tasks, relationships, etc. When you have that gut feeling in your stomach telling you to do something and you just don't want to do it - it's going to dwell in your mind until it gets done. This can lead to stress. Don't procrastinate, just do it.

K is for Kindness

A little kindness can go a long way. This is a word you'll hear all the time, and it may seem insignificant. But the power this small word carries is so important. A smile can change someone's day; a compliment can lift someone's spirit; a friendly, casual conversation can lead to a friendship. Even outside of school, kindness is important. Smile at the person you pass on the street, hold the door for others—the list goes on and on, and every action can be linked back to this one small word. Always show kindness to those around you, because the impact can be incredible.

L is for Listen

As much as you want to talk to the person beside you in class, you'll find that it's so much more important for you to listen. This rule goes for everything. Listen to your peers, family, teachers, etc. when they're talking to you. Listening shows others that you care. Sometimes people need to talk about their feelings as an emotional outlet. If it's you listening to what these people say, give them a genuine answer. Listening to others will get you far in life, so every once in a while you have to shut your pie hole and just listen.

M is for *Music*

When I started middle school, I was fortunate enough to feed into a fantastic band program that has helped to me to gain friends, go to incredible places, and gain a sense of therapy and knowledge from music. Music is something that helps many people to concentrate, express themselves, and find comfort and joy in. Whether you pursue music through playing an instrument, singing, or listening, music is an excellent way to connect with others and yourself.

N is for **Neatness**

Mess can be a huge mood killer. You may not even realize it until it's too late. When doing homework in a messy room or looking for a single paper in an explosion of them in a binder, it can easily lead to tension. A neat area with no clutter allows for breathing room and a clearer mind. Although it can be hard to keep something neat, there is one easy way to do it. DO NOT let the mess accumulate. If you pull something out of your notebook, put it back where it goes. Don't shove it back in in some random spot, because that will become a habit and end on lost, crumpled, and messy papers. In your room, keep items where they go and put them back if you get them out. Use binders at school and storage bins at home to keep a neat area. Trust me, a clean area equals a happy aura. Neatness makes it so much easier to focus on tasks and think clearly.

O is for Optimism

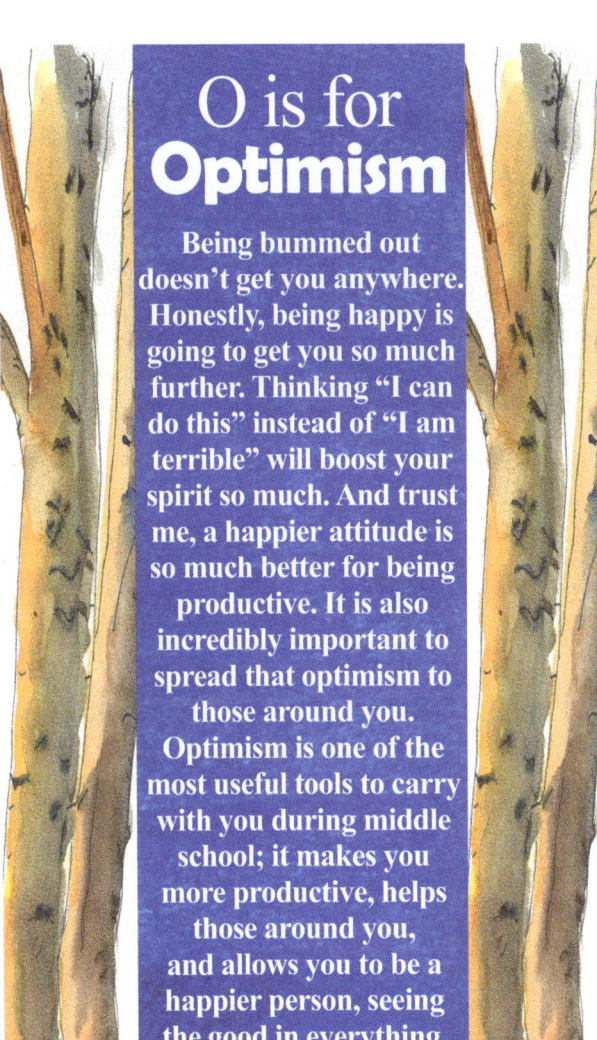

Being bummed out doesn't get you anywhere. Honestly, being happy is going to get you so much further. Thinking "I can do this" instead of "I am terrible" will boost your spirit so much. And trust me, a happier attitude is so much better for being productive. It is also incredibly important to spread that optimism to those around you. Optimism is one of the most useful tools to carry with you during middle school; it makes you more productive, helps those around you, and allows you to be a happier person, seeing the good in everything.

P is for **PUBERTY**

Don't you dare try to skip this page. I don't care whether you think you're a puberty mastermind or trying to avoid the awkwardness of this subject—this is very important. Puberty deals with acne, voice changes, and all sorts of things boys and girls deal with during middle school. It's totally normal to feel awkward when going through puberty, so just know that you're not alone. It's important to understand what your body is going through, you can do this by talking to your local pediatrician or guardian(s). If you feel uncomfortable talking about it, there are lots of other resources you can use such as books and reliable websites.

Q is for *Quotes*

I'll admit it—I'm a sucker for a good quote. There's something about the way you relate to a quote that is just special. We hear quotes daily—in movies, in books, from people in our everyday lives. You feel understood and get the sense that other people have been through the same thing and got through it. Quotes give you a sense of hope—encouragement that is such a beautiful gift to have.

R is for *Relationships*

Relationships are very important. With your friends, family, teachers, peers, significant other—they all hold great places in our lives. Respect the relationships in your life. Show gratitude to those who care for you. Love them—they have done so much for you. Take the time to thank them. Don't take healthy relationships for granted—appreciate them. You may believe that the love of your life is your boyfriend or girlfriend at the time, and they may be, but never lower your boundary level or morals for them unless you feel completely comfortable. To love someone else, you must first love yourself and know your worth.

S is for Stress

Ah yes, my good friend stress.
At one point or another we
all get stressed out. Stress is such an
unhealthy emotion but it can be defeated.
Make sure to hydrate, eat, exercise,
and rest as much as your body tells you
to. These essentials will help you to be less
stressed by giving you a healthy balanced
lifestyle. Remember that worrying is
useless and won't help anything.
When you're stressed out it tends to make
you think in a more negative way than
positive. When this happens,
talking to someone you trust and
going outside to breathe in some
fresh air can help to calm you.
As challenging as it may sound,
life is about doing what you're
passionate about and not
sweating the small stuff.

T is for Time Management

Our time is valuable, so always use it in the most productive way possible. Whether that time is spent taking a nap or on a run, it's important to recharge but also to use that energy to get done what you need to get done. Managing your time allows you to gain a sense of organization and figure out the things that mean the most in your life. In my experience, when I put homework, exercising, or even writing this book in the back of my mind I tend to get more stressed out because I haven't completed those things. Figuring out a schedule to accomplish what you need to get done can lead you to success and feeling a sense of pride and accomplishment.

U is for Understanding

Gaining a sense of an open mind and welcoming the chance to try to understand people is a challenging concept of life. People puzzle people. We find it hard to understand people's choices in life and sometimes even our own. To understand someone's choices we must put ourselves in their shoes and try to see from their perspective. We must do the same to understand someone's problem. When you genuinely understand what a friend or family member is going through, it can greatly help them to know someone is there for them and truly knows what they're going through.

V is for
Vulnerable

We all have a vulnerable side, some more than others. Though vulnerability can be scary and hard to handle, it's important to expose our vulnerable side because it allows you to get closer with others. To love, we must first risk being hurt. This allows us to be vulnerable and show others how we feel. We get in touch with our vulnerable sides by expressing our feelings. This is extremely important in any relationship you'll ever pursue.

W is for Worries

Worries tend to throw a dance party in our head making just enough noise to make it hurt. You have to believe me when I say this—it will be okay. You have to remember that you have total control of your body and mind. Worrying is absolutely useless. In no way will it help you. If you ever get overwhelmed by your worries take three deep breaths, try to settle your mind and relax. You can't change things that are out of your control, so let things happen and accept it. Worrying is a waste of time that will weaken you. Relax. Breathe. Settle. Accept.

X is for **X-ercise**

When I was in middle school I never worked out. I got home from school, watched a few episodes of Modern Family, did my homework, ate, then fell asleep. I felt drained of energy and that I had to follow this continuous pattern of living. Later I started playing softball for my school, and going from a girl who got out of breath walking up a flight of stairs to a two hour practice every day after school, was a huge challenge. Getting in shape is difficult but it pays off. Exercising can help to bring happiness to your life by releasing endorphins. If you're ever feeling sad, there are tons of workout videos all over the Internet that can help. So come on! Get up and do a few burpees.

Y is for
You Are Important

Out of everything in this book, I want to stress this more than anything. Every single one of you are priceless and absolutely irreplaceable. It doesn't matter what you've done, if you think you aren't good enough, if you hate what you see in the mirror—you are beautiful. So magnificently beautiful. There will never be anyone exactly like you, with your thoughts, feelings, heart, and mind. You can do so much and you each have something to offer the world. Learn to love yourself. Don't pick at your imperfections—accept them and see them as beautiful as art. You are a masterpiece. Never forget that someone cares and loves you, and always will.

Z is for
ZEROTOLERANCE

Middle school is a time where you or others may start to develop feelings for a special someone. It is not okay to make fun of someone for who they like or identify themselves as. Sometimes you feel like you're different than other people, but I'll let you in on another secret—that's how everyone else feels too. Don't judge them as you wouldn't want them to judge you. Remember that you wouldn't want to be discriminated against for believing, feeling, or thinking something different than others.

Bio

Aryelle Jacobsen currently attends AC Reynolds High School (class of 2018) in beautiful Asheville, North Carolina and lives with her mom, dad, brother, two dogs and hedgehog. She enjoys CrossFit, running, backpacking, traveling, marching band and spending time with her friends and family. She plans to study public health in college and hopes to someday open a school.

If you are an organization wishing to buy bulk quantities of this book, please contact Chiron Publications at generalmanager@chironpublications.com.

Resources

Bullying:
www.stopbullying.gov

Children with Special Needs:
PACER CENTER: Champions for Children with Disabilities and Health Information Center (including Family to Family Health Information Centers in each state)
www.pacer.org

Depression:

Crisis Call Center
800-273-8255 or text ANSWER to 839863
crisiscallcenter.org/crisis-services

Eating disorders:
National Eating Disorder Association
www.nationaleatingdisorders.org (800) 931-2237
Families Empowered and Supporting Treatment of Eating Disorders
www.feast-ed.org

Family Voices
www.familyvoices.org

LGBTQ+:
Parents, Families, and Friends of Lesbians and Gays (PFLAG)
www.pflag.org
Human Rights Campaign
www.hrc.org/campaigns/coming-out-center
Gay & Lesbian Alliance Against Defamation (GLAAD)
www.glaad.org
Scarleteen: www.scarleteen.com

Resources

Puberty:
kidshealth.org/en/kids/puberty.html
pbskids.org/itsmylife/body/puberty
Resiliency:
Youth Thrive Efforts through the Center for the Study of Social Policy at: www.cssp.org/reform/child-welfare/youth-thrive/Youth-Thrive-PPF-definitions.pdf
American Academy of Pediatrics:
www.fosteringresilience.com/7cs.php
Suicide prevention:
National Suicide Prevention Lifeline:
suicidepreventionlifeline.org
1-800-273-8255
It's Ok 2 Ask: www.itsok2ask.com
Sexual Assault
1-800-656-4673
www.rainn.org
Teen Substance Abuse:
www.al-anon.alateen.org/for-alateen 888-425-2666
www.teenaddictionanonymous.org/the12steps
www.addictioncareoptions.com 800-784-6776

A is for Awkward is a Girl Scout Gold Award project.

www.ingramcontent.com/pod-product-compliance
Lightning Source LLC
Chambersburg PA
CBHW041929040426
42444CB00018B/3471